Malaga
told to children

Text Francisco Bueno
Drawings Pilarín Bayés de Luna

Ediciones Miguel Sánchez

The cover depicts people from Malaga of many ages and kinds: artists, students, cigar makers, confraternity members, legionnaires with their figure of Christ... Among them can be seen the sculptor Jaime Pimentel, the lawyer Victoria Kent, the doctor Norman Bethune, the actor Antonio Banderas, the journalist Paco Pérez Bryan, the singer Luz Casal and the painter Pablo Picasso.

Translation: Babel Traducciones, s.l. (Charles Davis)

Photomechanics: Paperlitos, s.l.

Layout and final artwork: Susana Martínez Ballesteros

Printing: Gráficas La Madraza (Albolote, Granada)

Legal deposit: GR 1777-2022

I.S.B.N.: 978-84-7169-221-4

Printed in Spain

I'm going to tell you what Malaga was like in ancient times and what it's like now. It's a wonderful city that you will love getting to know.

It's situated at the centre of a bay surrounded by mountain ranges. Two rivers, the Guadalmedina and the Guadalhorce, flow through the city and out into the Mediterranean.

Malaga has three thousand years of history. Imagine! It's both old and new, so much so that everyone who visits it, from all over the world, falls in love with it.

It was founded by the Phoenicians in the eighth century BC, which makes it one of the oldest cities in Europe. They were the inhabitants of what is now Israel, Syria, Lebanon and Palestine, a region called Canaan in ancient times. As their land was sandy and barren, they concentrated on trade, travelling along the Mediterranean coasts in search of the things this land had to offer, to take them to their distant country. Their boats were small and slow, so they decided to found a kind of village in this beautiful bay. From the surrounding area they cut wood, caught and salted fish and gathered figs, raisins and other products to take them back to their homeland. Some of them, seeing how well they lived here, decided to stay for good.

The Phoenicians were the first to bring coins to our land. They used little pieces of silver and other minerals to pay for what they bought. We owe them the techniques of wine-making, so deeply rooted in our culture, as well as the ability to make use of land that was difficult to cultivate in mountainous terrain, which they exploited to the full through their ingenuity and hard work.

They were probably one of the first peoples to visit the Iberian Peninsula and bring us their culture. They were soon followed by others from the Mediterranean coasts, such as the Carthaginians or the Greeks themselves.

LIBANO
SRAEL
LESTINA

Roman Malaga

The years passed and the Romans, after endless struggles with the Carthaginians and the Greeks, took control of the countries surrounding the Mediterranean, and also occupied the Iberian Peninsula. They brought us many things. Their own language, Latin, remained with us permanently, adapted to each of the countries they invaded. This happened with Spanish, French, Italian and Portuguese, for example, all of them formed from Latin. They built countless cities, monuments, theatres, aqueducts, bridges, roads, and so on, but above all they left us their culture, which is now ours.

When they saw this lovely spot, they built a city, which they called *Malaca*. They even gave it their laws, and called the one they established here *Lex Flavia Malacitana*.

We still have something tangible left of them: a theatre, no less,

which we can see every day in our city. Because the Romans, and also the Greeks, were very fond of the theatre. The performances lasted all day and they put on tragedies and comedies to keep the audience entertained, sometimes with more serious stories and other times to laugh at things, real or invented.

The most spacious area was the tiered seating where the spectators sat. It was called the *caveas*, and was arranged in a semicircle so that the audience could hear the actors clearly. Between the tiered seats and the stage there was a space of about fifteen metres where the authorities sat. Then came the stage, where the actors declaimed their plays. In their own language, Latin, they called it the *proscaenium*. It is usually protected by a wall which served to enclose the theatre and helped the audience to hear the actors clearly.

Very close to the theatre we can see something that the Romans also left in Malaga: these are the **Garum Basins**, and I'll tell you what they were for.

One of the products most appreciated by rich Romans was manufactured in Malaga, which already back then was a city devoted to fishing. It was called *garum*, and was made from fish: they put anchovies, sardines, and heads and guts of other larger fish into those basins, mixed them with salt, wine, vinegar and water, and left it all there to macerate for a while. Then they took out the finished product, packed it in barrels and sent it to Rome, no less, where it was used as a sauce in foods, and was also said to cure many diseases. So there you have one of Malaga's sources of

wealth in Roman times, because it was produced in huge quantities, and the Romans relished this product.

During the period of Roman rule, Christianity reached Spain and spread in our country, becoming the majority religion. With Christianity came culture, leaving us great scholars and saints who are still the wonder of the world today.

Jewish Malaga

The Jews are a cultured, learned and hard-working people, but throughout their history they have always ended up being expelled from their places of origin. They came to Spain, which they called *Sepharad*, even before the Romans. They built neighbourhoods and synagogues and devoted themselves to medicine, trade and many other things. Some of them were so learned that they came to occupy very important positions.

In Malaga, in our Alcazabilla district, one of those highly influential Jews, called Samuel Negrella, had a spice shop. Then he moved to Granada and became the prime minister of the Granadan Zirid kings, between 1035 and 1055.

Another distinguished Jew, and one whose statue you can admire in a prime position in the Alcazabilla district, was Solomon ibn Gabirol, who liked to use the affectionate nickname "the Malagan" in his writings, because he was born here in 1021. He is probably the most important philosopher and poet ever born in this city. Later he moved to other cities and became even more famous.

You should know that the Malagan Jewish community is one of the most important in Spain nowadays.

Muslim Malaga

In the year 711 the Muslims invaded Spain. It was ruled at that time by the Visigoths, who, along with other peoples, had expelled the Romans centuries before. They gave Spain great scholars, but a hundred years later their monarchy was in a mess and society was an even greater mess. King Wittiza died and the nobles, to the great anger of his sons, chose Roderic. Wittiza's sons went to Ceuta in search of allies, and there they found the Muslims, who had just conquered North Africa and wanted to take over the world.

Sure enough, under the command of Tarik they crossed the Strait of Gibraltar, defeated Roderic and conquered Spain in a blitzkrieg. From then on they were masters of the Iberian Peninsula, or part of it, for nearly eight centuries. However, their rule in Al-Andalus, as they called this land, was far from peaceful. They were times of continuous wars, some with the Christian kingdoms which were gradually conquering territory from them to the north, and others with other Muslim peoples who invaded them from North Africa, to the south.

TARIK

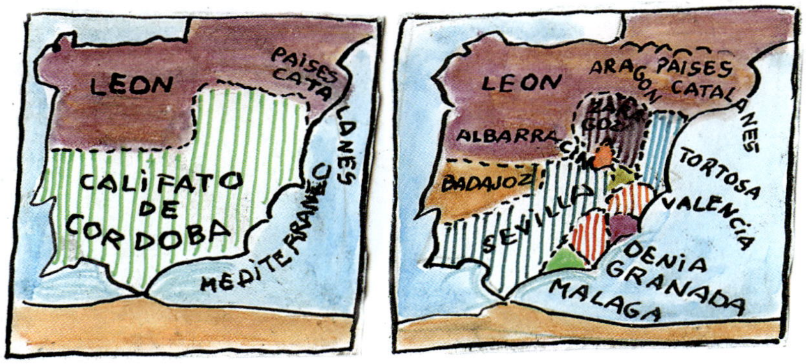

They reached their greatest splendour in the tenth century, with Abd-al-Rahman III, who founded the Caliphate of Cordoba, which at that time was one of the most important cities in the world. When the Caliphate fell in 1013, Muslim Spain was broken up into small *taifa* kingdoms, much weaker and more divided, constantly fighting among themselves. Little by little, they lost territory. By the thirteenth century all they had left in the Peninsula was the Nasrid kingdom of Granada, of which Malaga was one of the most important cities. But I'll tell you about that later.

Many things have come down to us from the Muslims and their culture. They left us buildings that dazzled the world, such as the Alhambra in Granada, the Mosque in Cordoba, the Aljaferia in Zaragoza, and many more. In Malaga we have two that are admired by those who see them: the Alcazaba and Gibralfaro.

The **Alcazaba** is both a palace and a fortress at the same time, apparently built on top of an earlier construction of Phoenician origin. What we see today was created gradually over the centuries, from the eleventh, the period of the *taifa* kingdoms, to the thirteenth, fourteenth and fifteenth centuries, when the kings of the Granadan Nasrid dynasty dominated the king-

dom. It was they who built it as it has come down to us today. After the conquest of the city, the Catholic Monarchs also ordered important alterations to be made in it. But you should be aware that a lot of what is now most attractive and

well preserved is a twentieth-century reconstruction, because the passing years left it in a bad state and for a time it was abandoned.

It is the prototype of medieval military architecture, with two large perimeter walls, one outer and one inner, imposing towers and as many as eight fortified and well guarded gateways that gave access to the various parts of the enclosure. From the lowest part of the wall, closest to the city, where the ordinary people lived, it rises to the highest area, which contained the palaces occupied by the king, his vizier or chief minister and the *qadi* in charge of governing Malaga.

I will also tell you that when it was rescued from its ruins and the archaeological remains began to appear, they were embellished with beautiful gardens. One of the prettiest is the one in the inner courtyard, with little water channels, a fountain in the centre and beautiful views of the sea and the city. From its archaeological remains we know that it also had a residential area with its houses arranged in small streets aligned with each other. These were probably the living quarters of the families that served the fortress and its rulers, or the elite guard under the command of the soldiers who watched over it.

In this high part, as I've already told you, are the palaces, heavily restored. To help you understand them better, I'll tell you that most Muslim houses that could afford it, even the smallest, had a rectangular courtyard, more or less large depending on their importance, containing a small pool. It was usually decorated with aromatic plants, lemon trees, vines, and so on. Around this patio were all the rooms of the house. We find the same layout, with beautiful patios, in these palaces.

They are from very different periods, as you can tell by their different decoration and style and even by the

shape of their arches. The first, the Taifa palace, is from the eleventh century. The second, the Nasrid palace, dates from the fourteenth century and consists of two dwellings, each with its patios and pools. It reminds you a lot of some spaces in the Alhambra. Do you know why? Well, because it was ordered to be made by Yusuf I, who ruled the kingdom of Granada between 1333 and 1354 and also built some of the most important palaces in the Alhambra. He was one of its most legendary kings, known as "the Great Emir".

This Alcazaba was where the kings of Granada stayed. Malaga was the economic and commercial capital of their kingdom. It was so beautiful and they liked it so much that they embellished it with buildings, scenic vistas, palaces and mosques.

Another of the Muslim buildings we have, so close to the Alcazaba that it's attached to it, is **Gibralfaro Castle**.

It seems, from archaeological remains that have been found, that there was already some sort of Phoenician construction on this site. Apparently, the Caliph of Cordoba, Abd-al-Rahman III, had a fortress built here. This castle and its surrounding walls, as we know them today, are the work of Yusuf I, although it was his son, Muhammad V, who finished it. Its name, *Gibralfaro*, means "hill of the lighthouse" in Arabic, because it had a lighthouse which showed sailors the direction they should take on dark nights.

It is above the Alcazaba, which made it the most difficult enclosure for the enemy to conquer and the last place from which to resist the attack, as happened in the siege of the city by the Catholic Monarchs. Yusuf I

joined it to the Alcazaba, connecting the two fortresses by a walled path which the Muslims called the *Coracha*. This made it easier for soldiers to pass safely from one fortress to the other, preventing the attacking army from dividing their defending forces.

The perimeter of the castle was protected by a double wall; around the inner wall runs the walkway along which the guards patrolled from tower to tower, of which there are now eight. Because of its height, this path around the wall has unique views of the city and its surroundings.

The castle is divided into two large areas. The lower one contains the inner bailey or courtyard, the stables, the barracks for the troops and the stores. In the upper part is the main courtyard, where there is now a very useful interpretation centre to help visitors understand this place. There is also the seventeen metre main tower or keep, which, as in all medieval castles, was the highest, where the commander of the garrison usually lived, built in the most difficult part of the fortress to conquer. In this upper area were also the baths and the Airón well, from the Phoenician period, forty metres deep, into which the underground water flowed. There were also cisterns for storing water. You must realise that

when a castle is built, one of the first jobs that has to be done is to provide it with its own water, because without this it would be impossible to resist a siege.

As you will now see, in this strategic location of Gibralfaro the bravest Muslims managed to hold out without surrendering, even days after King Ferdinand had captured the entire city of Malaga.

Christian Malaga

As I told you before, the Christians gradually came together over the centuries to form larger and larger kingdoms and succeeded in conquering almost all the territory of what is now Spain. By the thirteenth century the only part that the Muslims had left under their control was the Nasrid Kingdom of

Granada. This kingdom extended over more than half of present-day Andalusia. Malaga was the second most important city after Granada, its capital.

Well, in 1478 the Catholic Monarchs, Isabella and Ferdinand, who had managed to unify the whole of Christian Spain through their marriage, prepared their armies for this momentous event in our history. The first thing they did was to send an ambassador to the King of Granada, Muley Hacen, inviting him to surrender. But Muley Hacen, who was very fierce and cruel, got very angry and was on the point of killing the ambassador in his rage. From then on, each side launched a series of attacks, but the main battle, the hardest and cruellest, was the conquest of Malaga in 1487, and now I'll tell you about it.

By this time, the ruler in Granada was Boabdil, who was given two nicknames: some called him "the Little King", because he was small in stature, and others "the Unfortunate", because as soon as he was born a fortune-teller said that he would not be happy and would lose the kingdom. He had overthrown his father, Muley Hacen, who was a bad person and was already old. Boabdil did not have everything his own way, because some people were for him and others against. The more hardline faction couldn't stand him and preferred his father. And the toughest of them, almost all from the Gomeres tribe, came to live in Malaga, including the most terrible, Hamet el Zegri, who shut himself in Gibralfaro Castle with a large band of soldiers as fanatical as himself.

The Christian army, commanded by King Ferdinand, came from Velez-Malaga, a city that had just surrendered to him. There were a lot of soldiers and they were very well armed. But the decisive weapon that enabled the Christians to achieve victory was enormous artillery pieces that fired large stone or iron balls capable of piercing the walls of the city and its castles. They were called *bombards*, and as there were no roads, they were brought from Velez-Malaga by boat.

The king sent messengers to Malaga to tell them that if they surrendered their lives would be spared, but encouraged by el Zegri they said they would fight to the death. Then the Christian army surrounded the city and began to fire the bombards, knocking down its walls and killing and terrifying everyone.

There was a group of merchants in the city who didn't want war but wanted to surrender to the Christians, because they thought that by doing so they could at least save their lives. They were led by a merchant named Ali Dordux, who went up to Gibralfaro every day to talk to el Zegri and tell him to surrender, but el Zegri refused to give in and was determined to fight to the end.

The battle lasted for several months and many soldiers died on both sides. El Zegri's Moors were fierce and the Christians were so surprised and frightened that many of them told King Ferdinand that it was best to leave them alone and go home. But the king, who was very stubborn, not only told them that the conquest had to be completed, but also asked Queen Isabella to come from Cordoba, where she was at the time, to witness the siege and final capture of the city.

When she arrived, the queen was astonished at the beauty of Malaga. As she was very curious, she wanted to see her soldiers at close quarters, as well as the walls, and even the interior of the city, and a meal was prepared for her at the place now known as Monte Sancha, from which everything could be seen. When el Zegri saw her retinue, he tried to take revenge by sending soldiers to attack the queen. Naturally they were repelled by the Christians, who killed many of them.

Finally, on 13 August 1487, with the help of merchants and ordinary people who opened the gates to them, Malaga was conquered by the Catholic Monarchs. El Zegri, in spite of everything, would not surrender and remained entrenched with his Gomeres in Gibralfaro, from where he had to be removed by force, because otherwise he would not leave. Some of the rebels were expelled, others were sold as slaves and others left for Africa, but most died.

On 18 August the Catholic Monarchs entered the city in triumph, freed the Christian captives held there and left a garrison to defend it. What the Muslims called the "hand and mouth" of the Kingdom of Granada was now

in Christian hands, because through Malaga came money, horses and men from African tribes that they would no longer have. Just four years later, with the surrender of Granada, the conquest of Spain by the Christians was complete.

The most important work of architecture undertaken after the conquest was the **Cathedral**.

A few days after taking the city, the Catholic Monarchs ordered it to be built on the site where the great mosque previously stood. It was to be the newly conquered city's Cathedral Basilica of the Incarnation. The original design was by Diego de Siloé, architect of the cathedrals of Granada and Guadix, the church of St Jerome in Granada and the church of the Saviour in Ubeda, among others. The famous architect Andrés de Vandelvira was also involved later.

As it took so many years to build, several styles can be seen in it. Some parts are Renaissance, others Baroque, and in others the Gothic style is to the fore. The result is this great cathedral, visible from any point in the city, full of history, which opened to the public, still without its towers, in 1768. The great main entrance is Baroque in style. The North Tower rises to a height of eighty-seven metres, and it is the highest cathedral in the whole of Andalusia. One tower is missing, as it was originally designed with two, and for this reason it is known as "la Manquita" ("the one-armed lady"). It is said that the money to build that tower was sent to North America to finance its War of Independence, in which, by the way, another distinguished native of Malaga named Bernardo de Gálvez played a decisive role.

We can admire the nave and side aisles, the beautiful high altar, the extraordinary choir by Pedro de Mena, who created the figures attached to the backs of the seats, making

BERNARDO DE GALVEZ
1528
1782

PEDRO de MENA
VIRGEN DEL ROSARIO
VIRGEN DE LOS REYES
RETABLO GÓTICO
TANTUM ERGO
TANTUM ERGO

it one of the most important sets of sculptures in Spanish Baroque art. The chancel, the magnificent painting of the Virgin of the Rosary by Alonso Cano, the popular Virgin of the Monarchs and the old Gothic altarpiece of St Barbara make this cathedral worth visiting: a place that instils peace and serenity and invites you to pray.

Present-day Malaga

Now let's get to know Malaga as it is today. It's the most beautiful, the most magnificent of cities, the Malaga of the present with its clean streets, squares, museums and port.

Let's have a look at the Plaza de la Merced.

This is a beautiful rectangular square. It was the place where the Catholic Monarchs rescued el Zegri's Christian captives. Now its buildings are modern, but not very. In the centre stands an obelisk, with benches around it on which young and old sit and chat in this city's unique sunshine.

At the time of the conquest this square was outside the city walls. Later on a beautiful church was built here; it was burnt down in 1931. The obelisk in the centre commemorates General Torrijos, who fought to drive the French out of Spain and to defend the democratic Constitution of 1812 against those who wanted to impose tyranny. In the end, the bad people killed him on the beaches of Malaga along with forty-eight soldiers accompanying him. They are buried under here.

1931-39
1 PTA
REPUBLICA ESPAÑOLA
MALAGA 1939-1975
2 PTAS
ESPAÑA
MALAGA 1975
ESPAÑA
MALAGA
REINO DE ESPAÑA
20 CTS
ALFONSO XIII
ESPAÑA
MALAGA
MALAGA 2022
MALAGA
ESPAÑA
NAPOLEON BONAPARTE
GENERAL
TORRIJOS
TORRIJOS
1812
siglo XX
1812

Picasso

And in this square Pablo Picasso, probably the most famous painter of the twentieth century, was born. Just nearby is the Calle Granada. It's narrow, full of old mansions, modern houses, bars and shops selling knick-knacks and souvenirs for tourists, as if it wanted to take us from past centuries to the best of the present. In an alley very close to here is what was once the Palace of the Counts of Buenavista, which now houses the museum that Malaga has devoted to Picasso, its most brilliant painter. Let me tell you a bit about his life.

Pablo Ruiz Picasso was born in Malaga on 25 October 1881. His father was a drawing teacher who liked pigeons and bullfights, and the son inherited those tastes from the father, also learning the technique of painting. When he was a bit older he left for Barcelona and Paris, where he established himself as the best painter of the twentieth century. If he was sad he painted in blue. Then he fell in love and painted everything pink. Later on he began to break down forms in a style that made him famous and became known as cubism. But Picasso knew the world as children know it. That's why he painted so many pictures with clowns, circuses and acrobats. I could almost tell you that he painted like a child. This museum is a source of

pride to the people of Malaga and of admiration to many Spanish and foreign people who visit it.

Once we are inside we can admire the works on display, mostly paintings, with some beautiful pottery and sculptures.

Picasso was a great artist who painted constantly, so there are works by him in many places around the world. And besides this one, there are museums devoted exclusively to him in Paris, Barcelona, Coruña, Horta de San Juan and Buitrago de Lozoya. But I'm sure this is the

one he would like most because it's next to the square where he was born.

As well as this museum dedicated to Picasso, Malaga has many others, because one of the great treasures of this city is the number and variety of its museums, especially after the last few years. By visiting them we can be transported to other periods and explore the history of art and culture, from ancient archaeology to more modern paintings, sculptures and works.

And not only that: this city and its streets are like an open-air museum, with sculptures in every style and memories of a fascinating past.

Well, the next museum I want to tell you about is one of the favourites of the people of Malaga.

The "great" Museum of Malaga

This is situated in the beautiful Customs Palace, which was built in the eighteenth century in a neoclassical style and was until recently the headquarters of various public authorities. It was recently adapted to be used as a museum and more than 2,000 works of art are exhibited in it.

Here you can admire magnificent sculptures and other works by Pedro de Mena, Alonso Cano, Vicente Carducho, Zurbarán, Murillo, Ribera, Sorolla, Carlos de Haes and many others. There is also a remarkable collection of paintings by Malaga artists, such as Moreno Carbonero, Muñoz Degrain, and others, and also some works by Picasso. In addition, the museum houses over 15,000 archaeological pieces from the eighth century BC to the Middle Ages.

The Carmen Thyssen Museum

This museum, containing Baroness Carmen Thyssen's private collection, is situated in a beautiful sixteenth-century Renaissance building, the Villalón Palace. It would not exist today without the generosity of this great woman, but she and her devotion to painting are linked to the figure of her husband. I'll tell you a bit about him.

Baron Hans Heinrich von Thyssen-Bornemisza was born in The Hague in 1921 and died in San Feliu de Guíxols in 2002. A great businessman and a distinguished member of one of the most powerful European families of industrialists, owners of more than 200 companies, he is remembered today as a patron. He and his father put together the fabulous pri-

vate collection of ancient, modern and contemporary art that is considered the most important of the twentieth century.

In 1985 he married the Spanish former actress Carmen Cervera, who from that day became Baroness Thyssen. Fortunately for all Spaniards, she arranged for her husband, after lengthy negotiations, to transfer his fabulous collection of paintings to the Spanish State. Thanks to this agreement it is exhibited and preserved in Spain, at the Thyssen Museum in Madrid, one of the most important and popular art galleries in the world.

In the years she spent with her husband and since his death, Baroness Carmen Thyssen has devoted her life and a large part of her fortune to assembling her own collection of paintings, the one we can now admire at the Carmen Thyssen Museum in Malaga.

It is an important collection of 285 works by Spanish and Andalusian painters from the nineteenth to the early twentieth century, from Goya to Picasso. Hanging on the walls we can admire a full range of subjects:

magnificent portraits, splendid landscapes and genre scenes that will also delight children, especially those keenest on painting.

As soon as we enter the port we run straight into another great museum:

Malaga Pompidou Centre

In 1969, Georges Pompidou, president of the French Republic, ordered a completely new large museum to be built in Paris, devoted to modern art. When it was finished, the authorities of that country decided to name it after him. Years later, Malaga City Council and the Paris Pompidou Centre came up with the idea of creating a branch of the French museum here.

It has many Spanish and foreign visitors, who marvel at how lovely the works on display are. Its location is very easy to find. The building, known in Malaga as "the Cube", with its striking shape and colouring, is very close to the sea, between the Palmeral de las Sorpresas

and Muelle 1, and it has become a symbol of the city. If you visit it, you'll love it.

Also admirable is the

Russian Museum of St Petersburg

The building is large, spacious, attractive, surrounded by flowers on one side and by the sea on the other. It was built in 1920 to house a former tobacco factory, which is why it is now known as the Tabacalera Building. And the City Council had a bright idea: to agree with the St Petersburg Museum to establish a branch here, to which they bring magnificent temporary exhibitions.

The Russians have fabulous artists. You can see works ranging from exquisite Byzantine icons to paintings, some small and others very large. They show the colouring of their land, sometimes cold and sometimes of lush beauty.

As I told you before, as well as those I've shown you, Malaga has many more museums, and is known for this all over the world: the Contemporary Art Centre, the Interactive Music Museum, another devoted to wine, another to religious confraternity art, another to honey, as well as those on the contemporary painters Revello de Toro and Jorge Rando and others on cars, fashion, glass, flamenco art... All of them, with their subject matter and their curiosities, make this city a place where it's impossible to be bored, where children and adults and everyone who visits it will always have something new to learn.

teatro romano
centro interpretación Gibralfaro
museo unicaja de artes y costumbres populares
museo de la imaginación
museo patrimonio municipal MUPAM
museo arte flamenco Peña J. Breva
museo vidrio y cristal
CLIN
Lagar de Torrijos
museo aeronáutico
La Concepción jardín botánico
museo basílica Santa María de la Victoria
TANTO MONTA
museo interactivo de música
museo & tour M.C.F.
principia centro de ciencia
Hispano Suiza
Biscuter
museo automovilístico y de la moda
FIAT
Ford
CHEVROLET
museo-tesoro de la cofradía de la expiación
INRI
museo de la archicofradía de la esperanza

Strolling around the city

In the very centre you'll find one of the most popular places to visit in Malaga today: Muelle 1 and the Palmeral de las Sorpresas. Until a few years ago the port was separated from the city by a fence, but today, luckily, this is no longer the case, as it has been connected to the city and integrated into it, producing these two wonderful spaces that are so well known and much visited.

They are places to stroll in and enjoy, gazing at hundreds of boats, some small, some larger, and others enormous cruise ships that leave thousands of tourists here every day.

If you're a bit tired of so many admirable works, you can opt for a change of scene and visit the beaches of La Malagueta to try the popular fried fish called *pescaíto*: small fresh anchovies known locally as "victorian", marinade, squid rings, skewered sardines, fried baby squid, which you'll probably be happy to enjoy. This is Malaga cuisine, which everyone likes so much, especially children.

From here you can watch the enormous cruise ships from which many tourists disembark. There are also cargo docks with hundreds of containers. And out at sea you can spot little fishing boats that bring large and small fish every day. Further off, sailing boats can be seen, and further still there are others, some of them commercial vessels,

ANA
POLICIA

others pleasure boats, seeming to mottle the endless sea on an enchanted afternoon.

Malaga is lovely whichever way you look at it. Very close to the sea is the beautiful Parque de la Alameda, proudly displaying ancient trees with a mass of multicoloured flowers. And there, within it, is the Casona del Parque (park mansion), where the mayor's office is and from where this city, which is lovelier and more welcoming every day, is run.

And very close to the Casona del Parque is Calle Larios, the busiest and most important street in the city, always brightly decorated.

There used to be traffic in this beautiful street, full of shops and bustle, until it was pedestrianised. It is a delightful place to stroll for locals and visitors. When the cruise ships arrive at the port stuffed with tourists, they walk up and down this street admiring its cleanliness, its architecture and the great abundance of places for relaxation that it contains. In the narrow adjoining streets there are many bars and restaurants where you can find delicious things to eat.

And what we can say about Holy Week, when it is more splendid than ever, all decorated with flags and crammed with people, with rows of chairs on either side? Solemnly and majestically, the great floats called "thrones" pass by, wonderfully decorated with flowers, carried by hundreds of bearers or "throne men", escorted by soldiers and many *cofrades* (confraternity members) and accompanied by bands playing melodies appropriate to the religious occasion. They process along the main streets of the city bearing extraordinary sculptures that represent the passion and death of Christ and arouse great devotion among the people. It is a visit you must not miss.

There are more things I could show you in Malaga, which enchants children and also parents and grandparents, because I want to tell you a secret: we grown-ups are also a bit like children and that's why we love this enchanted city.